Wonderful Word

POEMS OF PRAISE & WONDER

Written & Illustrated by
Dani Ruth Romero

Briley & Baxter Publications | Plymouth, Massachusetts

All Scripture in this publication is inspired by the Holy Bible, New
International Version ®, NIV ®

For information contact dani@rrillustration.com | www.rrillustration.com
Instagram: @ruthieromero_illustration

ISBN: 978-1-954819-63-4

DEDICATED TO ONE STONE NASHVILLE

The greatest church family a girl could receive...
Thank you to every person that has walked
with me on this journey,
Calling forth my God-given destiny,
Stewarding the artist He has called me to be...

A woman now alive in Christ
Full of hope & dreams
Rejoicing in who God has made her to be!

CONTENTS

CONTENTS CONTINUED

LAYiNG THE GROUNDWORK FOR
WONDERFUL WORD

Between the years of 2018-2019, I was doing a lot of explorative travel with the Lord—crossing the great seas and stepping foot on grounds I never dreamt I'd walk upon. From country to country, He was leading me all over the map!

As 2019 approached, I knew in my heart that God was asking me to go visit Nashville, Tennessee. As I gave Him my yes to His great invitation, unsure of how long I'd be staying there or what was in store, little did I know that God had a big surprise up His sleeve!

He began doing a great work within me, healing some of the deepest places of my heart, and showing me a love I have never experienced from Him before—a tangible, life-changing love. Unfolding a side of His nature like I've never seen, revealing His heart of pure kindness.

I took off my old lenses of the God I once "believed" He was, now understanding that God cared so much about me. He was yearning to restore my deepest hopes, and greatest desires. Through this transformative process, I wasn't expecting the restoration of my childhood dream of creating so-called "children's book illustrations." But as my heart healed, my creative inspiration subtly transformed into a whimsical, child-like style—the joyous fruit reflecting a season of further healing with Him.

Since I have embarked on this creative journey with my King, I am only seeing more of His heart each day. He surely is a God of Awe & Wonder and the ultimate restorer of dreams.

—Dani Ruth Romero

A GLORIOUS MISSION

In my quiet time with the Lord, both in moments of prayer & worship,
I would find my mind overflowing with creative imagery...
Knowing that this was not my own imagination,
But something that came like a gift from the King.

As I took the time to draw the things I'd see,
Various scripture would begin to flow within me simultaneously.
Little did I know that the Lord was creating & weaving together something so beautiful,
A tangible expression of my heart's worship,
Illustrated books coming to life, in a way to share with all mankind.

It is my greatest desire that these illustrated poems of praise & worship
Be a source of divine encouragement,
Stirring the hearts of not only children, but of all ages,
To seek more after the true heart of this incredible King,
Being free to receive all He has in store with child-like faith:
All hope & joy unleashed for those who believe.

Oh, wait!
One more thing....
Last but not least,
I pray that this book will open eyes to see the Bible in a new & exciting way,
Standing with a newfound awe & wonder of the living Word of God.

Thanks for reading!

—Dani Ruth Romero

WAYS OF WONDER

I long to see Your glory,
For You are a planet-rocking God!
How infinite are the marvelous things that You do?

What no eye has seen,
Are the things You have in store for me.

I want to see the kingdom way.
I want to trust You like never before.

A heart wide open, full of expectancy,
That You will do wonders beyond imagination
Only for my good.

How You always come through in impossible ways,
For those who trust in You with all their hearts.

I'm so excited to see Your paths of wonder.
I say yes to Your kingdom way!

Inspired Scriptures: 1 Corinthians 2:9, Job 5:9, Proverbs 3:5-6

ONE HAPPY HiPPO

With You, my Lord, is the abundance of life.
Nothing compares to Your great loving-kindness.
When I wake up, there is a fresh outpouring of new grace & love for me to walk in.
You see all of the smallest of details in the day ahead.
You know exactly what I need, when I need it.

Because of Your great love, I will not be consumed by the burdens that come my way.
You promise that You will meet all my needs, according to Your amazing riches!
You are the richest of all!

I don't need to worry about tomorrow, but rather seek You first & Your way of living,
& all the things I need will be given to me by You.
You care so much that You know the number of hairs on my head.
& Your thoughts about me are more than the grains of sand
Thank You for caring about every detail of my life!
I praise You because I am so magnificently made!

Inspired Scripture: Psalm 16, Lamentations 3:22, Philippians 4:19,
Matthew 6:33, Luke 12:7, Psalm 139

A MAJESTIC RIDE WITH THE KING

My faithful God,
A loving friend,
There is so much behind closed doors You desire to show me.

When I call on Your name,
You will unfold great & majestic things,
The things that people can't even begin to dream.

When I spend time with You,
You expand my mind to receive Your kingdom thoughts,
Filling me with Your hope,
Giving me eyes to see things the way You see,
Looking above & not beneath.

You revive my imagination,
Giving me excitement to explore new things.

I desire to spend more time with You each day,
Because it is here in Your presence
I experience a love I have never received,
A love that I can never begin to explain.

Maybe one day I can express how deep, wide, & high Your love is for me!
But right now in this moment, I will give thanks & praise to my King,
For filling me with more life than I could ever dream.

Inspired Scripture: Jeremiah 33:3, Colossians 3:2,
Psalm 23:2, Ephesians 3:18-19

JOY RIDE

All Your ways are glorious, Lord.
Who can compare with You?
There are no limits,
Nor are there borders,
To Your great & unfailing wonder.

You make Your great light shine on the darkest of places.
Please lead me on Your straight & narrow path.
Though it is the road less traveled & very few find it,
Great is the prize of following You!

Unexpected doors of excitement & adventure,
Rare treasure hidden in Your secret places.

I desire to walk on Your path of wonder,
Doing Your way of living.
For Your ways of wisdom are avenues of cheer & favor,
Leading to a peace I cannot describe.

I desire to see You work in impossible ways in my life,
Walking hand in hand with You, my faithful guide,
On this incredible joy ride!

Inspired Scripture: 2 Corinthians 4:6–12, Proverbs 3:17, Matthew 7:13

A GLORiOUS PERSPECTiVE

Oh Lord,
How mindful are You of all creation!
How considerate & detailed You are...
How long did it take You to count all of the stars,
Giving them each a name?

Out of Your glorious riches You pour out Your life-giving spirit!
It makes me believe for my deepest of hopes & dreams.

You awaken my heart to see things from Your higher,
More magnificent perspective.
Giving me greater faith to believe,
That with my God, anything is possible!

You are the only one who can open doors that no man can shut.
I long to bring glory to Your name!

Inspired Scripture: Psalm 147:4, Ephesians 3:16, Colossians 1:9–10

DINO WONDER

An unending promise You have made to me,
That You will never stop doing good to me.
A future & a hope You have given me.

How abundant are the marvelous things You have in store for me?!
You delight in every detail of my life.
What a wondrous King You are!

When I struggle in life & have my fair share of hard things,
You always remind me that You will be faithful to show me the way.
Constantly guiding me to wonderous things,
It's Your greatest joy to lead me by surprise.

I thank You, my King,
For always going far beyond my wildest dreams!!

Inspired Scripture: Jeremiah 32:40-44, Jeremiah 29:11,
Psalm 32:11, Psalm 35:27, Isaiah 30:20–21

TASTE & SEE

Our faithful Lord, how You are so good to Your creation!
Whether it be man or monkeys,
You love to shower us in Your affection.
You rejoice when we look to You for all we need.

How Your loving care causes us to dance & sing!
Knowing that when You open Your hand,
You will satisfy us more than the richest of treats.

For You are our God of abundance,
We will always praise You for meeting all of our needs & more!

Inspired Scripture: Psalm 145:15-16, Psalm 147:9,
Psalm 104:29, Psalm 63:3-5

LE MAGNiFiQUE ARTiSTE (THE MAGNiFiCENT ARTiST)

Lord, You are the master artist,
The Supreme Fashionista!
Everything I see, hear, touch & smell,
Are the things You have made.

There is no escaping Your creative goodness!
Even if I took off to space,
I would still see Your works of art:
The infinite stars You painted on the canvas of Your skies,
All radiating Your majestic light.

You say that I am Your masterpiece,
Your greatest work of art.
The human race is the crown of Your creation,
A step below Your angelic beings.

I thank You for creating me with a unique design & purpose,
Knowing one day I will fulfill all the good works You planned for me long ago!

Inspired Scripture: Ephesians 2:10, Psalm 8:3-6

PiZZA PRAiSE

We praise You,
Our master chef!
For always going above & beyond,
To satisfy our every need.

A delicious invitation You give me each day,
To taste & see that You are good,
How all creation can trust in Your devoted care.

You feed us from Your overflowing kitchen,
Serving up pizza that's out of this world.
No one compares to Your delectable goodness.

What no eye has seen,
Nor mouth tasted,
Is what You have in store for we who place our hope in You.

We praise You for pizza!
We praise You for Your delectable goodness!

Inspired Scripture: Psalm 34:8, 1 Corinthians 2:9, Psalm 36:6–9

OUR RADIANT KING

I praise You, my amazing King!
When I was sad & disheartened,
You turned Your ear to my cry.
You took me out of that gloomy place,
Lifting me to a place I could never dream...

A secret place,
One You desired to show me.
Though it seemed a little dark at first,
The glittering stars flooded the skies with Your majestic light.

How can it be, my creative King?
That You turn even the darkest of places into light?
How You illuminate my path to dance upon the clouds with You!

I praise You for Your overwhelming goodness,
My Glorious King.
The galaxies & stars will bow at Your feet
& dance in Your light!

We celebrate Your supreme goodness,
The one who made every living thing.
Thank You for Your radiant light.

Inspired Scripture: Nehemiah 9:6, Psalm 139:12, Psalm 40:1–3

THE GREAT MISSION

I praise You,
My God of might & power.
When obstacles rise,
You enable me to tread the heights,
Pouring out Your strength upon me to endure the distance.

It is not by my might nor power,
But by Your spirit that causes me to soar.
By Your grace alone do I move to higher places,
Breathtaking views along this journey.

You make me eager to explore new places,
Giving me boldness & courage to face my fears,
Embracing all of the adventures with You.

You say to walk by faith & not by sight,
For with Your help I can do all things.

You have given me a great assignment,
To follow You in all that I do.
How You will be with me wherever I go,
I give thanks & praise to You!

Inspired Scripture: Matthew 28:16-20, Joshua 1:9,
2 Corinthians 5:7, Habakkuk 3:19

JOY SLIDE

Oh Lord, we give thanks & praise to You.
How You are the source of our joy,
Always bringing color to our lives.

Nothing can compare with You,
Our extraordinary King.
How numerous are the wonders You have accomplished?
If I were to count them, I'd lose track!
Infinite are the awesome plans You have in store for our lives.

Help us to slide into the things You desire us to receive.
Expand our mind to dream wider,
Hoping higher than ever before.

You love when we are free to enjoy You,
Our limitless King!

Inspired Scripture: Psalm 40:5

DISCO PRAISE

Praise Him, You sun, moon & stars!
Let us disco under His majestic light!
For He wears a robe of majesty &
Clothes us in garments of praise.

Praise Him in the morning.
Praise Him at night.
Praise while You're eating or sleeping,
Because the battle is His to fight.

So I say, get up!
Dance for Joy!
Wanna know the secret to a good life?
Praise Him!
Offer Him lips of praise & thanksgiving!

Sing of Your hope,
In all of His impossible ways.
Discoing under His majestic light.

Inspired Scripture: Psalm 93:1, Isaiah 61:3, Hebrews 13:5

SEATED IN HIGH PLACES

Who is this King of Glory?
What does that even mean?

By just speaking a word,
This King created the heavens & the earth.
How can that be?

The sun, moon, & stars praise Him,
Reflecting all of His glory.
They all bow down to give honor to His name.

You are such a powerful & mighty King,
Yet You still consider me in all You do.
How can this be?

Because of Your great love for me You gave me Jesus,
Seating me in the heavenly places with Him,
Where I am forever safe & well-cared for by You.

It's Your greatest desire to give many good gifts.
May all see how rich Your kindness is toward Your children,
The ones who believe in Your name.

Inspired Scripture: Psalm 148:3-6, Psalm 24:8,
Ephesians 2:4-6, Psalm 33:6, Matthew 7:11

So PERFECT iN you

Good morning!
It's a new day.
As I rise, approaching that marvelous mirror,
I am so happy to see what I see:
A beautiful person made by the Greatest King!

When I get ready for my day, You gently say,
"You are beautiful my darling, so beautifully made!"

But what is beauty to You?
For it is a gentle & quiet spirit,
These are so precious in Your sight.

You clothe me in Your love,
& ask me to wear a heart of kindness & compassion,
Reminding me to keep humility & gentleness in my pocket.

How You created me in Your grand image.
I desire to be Your image bearer,
Making You a proud Father!
Thank You for making me just as I am!

Inspired Scriptures: Song of Songs 4:1, Psalm 17:15,
1 Peter 3:4 , Colossians 3:12-14

RESTING IN YOUR PROMISES

I receive Your invitation today,
To rest in all You are,
& all of Your peaceful promises.

I choose to fix my thoughts on You.
It's You alone that brings comfort to my soul.
By resting in all that You are, I am renewed.

Today my loving Lord, I will say yes to being quiet in You,
Trusting that You will move mountains,
When I simply rest in You.

Inspired Scriptures: Isaiah 30:15, Hebrews 3, Philippians 4:8-9

A LIGHT FOR ALL TO SEE

Just as You named all the stars in the sky,
So You called me by name.
I did not choose You, but You chose me,
To reflect Your glorious goodness,
Uniquely crafting me in Your image.

How You chose me to be a light to the nations,
To share the good news about my planet-rocking God!

Proclaiming that whoever follows You will never walk in darkness...
Because You are the light of life.

You are the Lord of all; that is Your name!
You will never give Your glory to any other person or thing.

Inspired Scriptures: Isaiah 42:6–9, John 8:12

CONSIDERING YOU

I come in the quiet,
Inclining my ears to hear Your still small voice.
How You come in both the big & small.

The galaxies display Your splendor,
& earthquakes show Your power...

But even the gentle blow of the wind can speak of Your love.
Your soft whisper means more to me than anything else,
Allowing me to know that You are close by.

You draw me in with such a deep intimacy I can't even begin to describe.
It's here in this place that You give me greater ability to abide.
Focusing my mind on things that are so lovely & true...
Things that are so worthy of You.

You have my full attention, Lord.
You have all of my heart.
Speak so softly to me about the things that matter to You.
How I love to abide in You!

Inspired Scripture: Psalm 131:1, 1 Kings 19:11-13, Philippians 4:8-9

SWEET SLEEP

You circle me around like a cozy blanket,
Laying Your gentle hand on me,
Infusing me with Your comfort.

I quiet my mind & heart.
I will be still & know that You are my God,
Taking rest in the shadow of Your wings.

As I dwell here in You,
You promise my sleep will be sweet,
Immersing me in Your peace.

It is here with You that I feel so safe,
Excited to dream the night away with You.

I thank You, my Great King,
For protecting me while I sleep.

Inspired Scriptures: Psalm 139:5, Psalm 46:10 ,
Proverbs 3:19-24, Psalm 4:8, Psalm 91:1-8

PEACEABLE TREATS

What a miracle working God You are!
You always make a way for me,
Giving me everything I need for a godly life.

You always keep a close eye on me,
Faithful to protect my every step,
Always making sure that I get where I need to be.

As I make You my life's focus,
You cause my enemies to be nice to me.
Sometimes they even bring me treats in peace!

Because I have made You my hope,
You open doors for me that no man can shut,
& give favor in the sight of all,
So I can step into the things You have planned for me.

I love You, my Victorious King.
Show me more of the adventurer You created me to be,
Formed in the image of my wondrous King!

Inspired Scripture: Proverbs 3:1-4, 2 Peter 1:3,
Proverbs 16:7, Revelation 3:18, Psalm 31:19

YOUR SHIMMERING LIGHT

Lord, You say I am the righteousness of God.
You desire me to do things Your way,
Which is the right way.
You love when my attitude reflects You,
Responding with soft & gentle answers to others.
You love when I serve with a humble heart,
& seek the best for others.

You delight when I serve without a grumbling mood,
Because when I do, I shine like a star in the sky,
Radiating the goodness of who You are for all to see.

You take me from glory to glory,
Causing my heart to look more like Yours.
Thank You for Your grace & patience toward me.
I long to love more like You,
Reflecting Your shimmering light,
Just like Your stars in the sky.

Inspired Scripture: Proverbs 15:1, 2 Corinthians 5:21, Philippians 2:14-16

A Victorious Song

My spirit sings to You,
Strength for today & hope for tomorrow,
For this is the great melody of my heart.
How Your heavens declare Your breathtaking beauty!
Day by day,
Night by night,
The galaxies display the work of Your hands.
The milky way shines Your outstanding wonder.
I find great joy & excitement as I discover Your mysterious ways.

I make music from my heart,
Because My victory comes from You.
For You are my strength & my song!

Inspired Scripture: Psalm 19:1, Exodus 15:1-2, Ephesians 5:19

HONEYMOON DREAM

Oh Lord,
It's too good to be true!
Life is like a honeymoon with You,
A place of pure bliss.
Getting lost in Your love,
Enjoying every single moment here with You.

My eyes are locked in Your gentle gaze,
Smiling in awe & wonder of my sweet King.

Your words are like honey—so sweet to my soul.
I never want to leave this place,
This honeymoon dream,
Where I stand face to face,
With a King who knows my name.

When I grasp the light of the world,
All darkness has to leave.
For I am now free to journey beyond the galaxies.
Dazzling heights are in store for me!

I will dance & sing with the moon & stars,
Praising of all of Your goodness,
On this honeymoon dream.

Inspired Scripture: Psalm 119:103, Jeremiah 15:16, Psalm 19:8-10

A DiSCO BALL HEART

To the One who made the moon & the stars,
You love to take the most broken things,
Making them more beautiful than ever before.

Oh, how You did that with me!
You saw my broken heart,
It was completely shattered...
All of the pieces were scattered.

All You required was my surrender,
Excited to show me what only You could do.

How You took all those fragmented pieces,
Gently sculpting something completely new.
Behold, a disco ball You made!
A piece that reflects Your light.

The way You came through for me,
It's more than I can express or contain.
Some call it beauty for ashes,
Or a joy unspeakable...

All I can do is dance before You,
Under Your beaming light.
Singing a song of Your healing love,
Telling of the great restorer You are.

Some of Your greatest creations are those that come from broken things,
Just like my disco ball heart.

Inspired Scriptures: Psalm 51:16-17, Psalm 8:3-6, Isaiah 61:1-3

More from Wonderful Word by Dani Romero

PRAiSE & WONDER
Coloring Book Edition

Deepen your walk with God through art! This coloring book for kids, teens, and adults includes 40+ single-sided unique illustrations that celebrate the glorious characteristics of God. All pages are inspired by scripture. The whimsical designs will be beloved by children and make adults feel childlike again. This coloring book incorporates the following themes:

God's miraculous ways
God as a healer and restorer for His people
God as an artist
God's gifts of hope and joy
God as our protector
The peace of God that surpasses all understanding
God's wonderful plan for His children
God as our victory and strength
God's promise of abundant life